REPORT

Communications Networks to Support Integrated Intelligence, Surveillance, Reconnaissance, and Strike Operations

Elham Ghashghai

Prepared for the United States Air Force

Approved for public release; distribution unlimited

RAND PROJECT AIR FORCE

The research reported here was sponsored by the United States Air Force under Contract F49642-01-C-0003. Further information may be obtained from the Strategic Planning Division, Directorate of Plans, Hq USAF.

Library of Congress Cataloging-in-Publication Data

Ghashghai, Elham.
    Communications networks to support integrated intelligence, surveillance, reconnaissance, and strike operations
/ Elham Ghashghai.
      p. cm.
    "TR-159."
    Includes bibliographical references.
    ISBN 0-8330-3664-5 (pbk.)
      1. Command and control systems—United States. 2. United States—Armed Forces—Communication systems.
I. Title.

UB212.G49 2004
355.3'3041'0973—dc22

                        2004018245

The RAND Corporation is a nonprofit research organization providing objective analysis and effective solutions that address the challenges facing the public and private sectors around the world. RAND's publications do not necessarily reflect the opinions of its research clients and sponsors.

RAND® is a registered trademark.

Published 2004 by the RAND Corporation
1776 Main Street, P.O. Box 2138, Santa Monica, CA 90407-2138
1200 South Hayes Street, Arlington, VA 22202-5050
201 North Craig Street, Suite 202, Pittsburgh, PA 15213-1516
RAND URL: http://www.rand.org/
To order RAND documents or to obtain additional information, contact
Distribution Services: Telephone: (310) 451-7002;
Fax: (310) 451-6915; Email: order@rand.org

Preface

U.S. military operations in the 21st century rely heavily on receiving and distributing information to and from the field of operation. Immense amounts of data must be collected, processed, and fused into knowledge via high-capacity networks. This report addresses the communications challenges associated with integrating current and future intelligence, surveillance, and reconnaissance (ISR) assets effectively with weapons platforms and the weapons themselves. It evaluates a variety of options for satisfying the needs of robust communications systems.

The research was sponsored by Major General Ronald F. Sams (Director, Intelligence, Surveillance, and Reconnaissance), Brigadier General Daniel Leaf (Director, Operational Requirements), and Mr. Harry Disbrow, all of whom report to the Deputy Chief of Staff of the Air Force, Air and Space Operations. The action officer was LtCol Karen Clark. This research was conducted within the Aerospace Force Development Program of RAND Project AIR FORCE as part of the "Integrated ISR-Strike" study led by Dr. Glenn Buchan. For further information, contact the author, Elham Ghashghai (310-393-0411, x7211; elham@rand.org).

RAND Project AIR FORCE

RAND Project AIR FORCE (PAF), a division of the RAND Corporation, is the U.S. Air Force's federally funded research and development center for studies and analyses. PAF provides the Air Force with independent analyses of policy alternatives affecting the development, employment, combat readiness, and support of current and future aerospace forces. Research is performed in four programs: Aerospace Force Development; Manpower, Personnel, and Training; Resource Management; and Strategy and Doctrine.

Additional information about PAF is available on our web site at http://www.rand.org/paf.

Contents

Figures

Tables

Summary

U.S. military operations in the 21st century rely heavily on receiving and distributing information to and from the field of operation. Immense amounts of data must be collected, processed, and fused into knowledge via high-capacity networks. The required high capacity in a hostile environment introduces significant challenges and conflicting requirements to the communications network for a variety of reasons.

The research in this report focuses on combat systems operating at medium and low altitudes, which pose different challenges from the challenges of intelligence, surveillance, and reconnaissance (ISR) platforms operating at high altitudes:

- Medium- and low-altitude airborne platforms, such as fighters and bombers, are closer to jammers and signals intelligence (SIGINT) receivers. Hence, the adversary systems may require less sensitivity to intercept those signals and less power to jam them.
- The low observability of the platforms can potentially be compromised by transmitting large amounts of data.
- During transmission of large amounts of data, platforms at lower altitudes are at a higher risk of being detected.

To fully understand the issues and challenges, we considered two types of threats: mobile jammers and SIGINT receivers able to detect and locate user transmitters. Such jammers and SIGINT receivers are hard to locate and engage. (See p. 5.)

We first discuss data requirements and threats and examine the current communications programs and shortfalls. We then analyze a variety of options in terms of frequencies, waveforms, and antenna types, and make suggestions for improving the current communications program based on altitude, range, data rate, and threat. (See pp. 11–15.)

The following are some of the main findings:

- The Joint Tactical Information Distribution System (JTIDS) and the future Joint Tactical Radio System (JTRS) do not have the required capacity to support a high-data-rate connectivity requirement. (See p. 6.)

- Common Data Link (CDL) family programs can provide a sufficient data rate for the fighter/bomber with Advanced Synthetic Aperture Radar System—Improved Program (AIP) capability. However, these systems need further improvement to survive a more severe threat environment. (See p. 21.)

- A near-term solution for improving jam resistance is the addition of nulling capability to CDL families (including Multiple Platform Common Data Link, MP-CDL). However, although nulling techniques are effective for jammers, they are not effective against SIGINT receivers that detect communications emissions. (See p. 22.)

- Agile, multibeam, low-sidelobe directional antennae are required to achieve more protection against jamming and intercept receivers. These techniques increase the size and weight of the antenna. (See p. 23.)

- The following communications options are effective against jamming and SIGINT detection but are not appropriate for medium- and low-altitude platforms. These options can be used for high-altitude platforms, such as ISR platforms, communications nodes, and satellites: (See pp. 21–29.)
    - Absorption band (55–60 GHz) is a viable option for links above 55 km (60 kft) because signals at absorption band get absorbed through the atmosphere. Absorption band is inherently effective against *ground* threats, but is not effective against *airborne* jammers and *airborne* SIGINT receivers.
    - Laser is the most robust option for links above 12 km (40 kft) because laser beams get absorbed through clouds.
    - Workarounds such as proliferated platforms, compression, alternative concepts of operation, and system augmentation (e.g., airborne relays) may be appropriate, but further analysis is needed to examine their effectiveness. In particular, proliferated platforms with multiple beams may form a more robust, reliable network.

In summary, there is no one solution for all situations and platforms. A combination of options will be needed for a reliable and robust communications link; these options may change depending on altitude, range, data rate, and threat. (See pp. 33–35.)

Thus, communications does not appear to be a major limiting factor, at least not technically, in developing future ISR forces. However, programmatic action will be required to develop the necessary systems, and the costs could be significant.

The communications problems posed by future ISR forces appear to be solvable, but at a cost.

The development of new systems, together with required platform modifications and new designs, raise technology and cost issues that are not addressed here but that need to be carefully examined.

Acknowledgments

The author would like to thank Glenn Buchan and Joel Kvitky for their guidance and inputs. She also would like to thank Robert Preston, Elwyn Harris, and Edgar Satorious for providing essential inputs and analysis to this work. This report greatly benefited from review comments from Ted Harshberger, Rosalind Lewis, Kristin Leuschner, Edward Bedrosian, and Carl Rhodes.

Acronyms

ABIT	Airborne Information Transmission
AESA	Active Electronically Scanned Array
AFRL	Air Force Research Laboratory
AIP	ASARS–Improved Program
ASARS	Advanced Synthetic Aperture Radar System
ATC	Automatic Target Cueing
CDL	Common Data Link
CNR	Carrier-to-Noise Ratio
CONOPs	Concept of Operations
CONUS	Continental United States
Eb/No	The required energy/bit-to-noise spectral density ratio (dB) to achieve a desired bit error rate
EO/IR	Electro-Optical/Infrared
ERP	Effective Radiated Power
ISR	Intelligence, Surveillance, and Reconnaissance
JTIDS	Joint Tactical Information Distribution System
JTRS	Joint Tactical Radio System
LPD	Low Probability of Detection
LPI	Low Probability of Intercept
MP-CDL	Multi-Platform Common Data Link
NCCT	Network Centric Collaboration Targeting
RF	Radio Frequency
SBR	Space-Based Radar
SIGINT	Signals Intelligence
SINCGARS	Single-Channel Ground and Airborne Radio System
SNR	Signal-to-Noise Ratio
TCDL	Tactical Common Data Link
TTNT	Tactical Targeting Network Techniques
UAV	Unmanned Aerial Vehicle

1. Introduction

U.S. military operations in the 21st century rely heavily on receiving and distributing information to and from the field of operation. Immense amounts of data must be collected, processed, and fused into knowledge via high-capacity networks. This report addresses the communications challenges associated with integrating current and future intelligence, surveillance, and reconnaissance (ISR) asset capabilities with weapons platforms and the weapons themselves.

The current research builds on our previous study of communication options for high-altitude platforms (it is now in preparation for publication). This phase of the research extends the overall communications network requirements to support the transport of high-throughput sensor data from medium- and low-altitude platforms via communications and/or ISR platforms to the processing and analysis centers located in the continental United States (CONUS).

The current study first examines the components of today's communications network and the capabilities and vulnerabilities inherent in both existing programs and those planned for the future. We then discuss the challenges that must be addressed and recommend solutions for increasing the survivability and resilience of the required communication links. The study focuses on technical solutions and not on other issues such as management, interoperability, spectrum allocation, or cost.

We look at two distinct kinds of threats: jamming and signal detection (the ability to "see" the enemy by receiving electromagnetic signals). These threats work in different ways. Jamming is directed at the *receiver* and consists of transmitting suitable waveforms to prevent or otherwise interfere with the receiver's ability to receive an intended communication. In contrast, detection is directed at the *transmitter* as an enemy signals intelligence (SIGINT) receiver attempts to "observe" and possibly gain information from the communication signals in order to locate the transmitter. Because they only receive signals, these threats are silent.

Although we lay out options for a survivable communications network to support whole-theater operations, our focus is on the survivability of the subset of the network that supports the transmission of sensor data from medium- and low-altitude platforms. This problem presents a more challenging case compared to high-altitude ISR platforms for a variety of reasons:

- Medium- and low-altitude airborne platforms are at a closer range to jammers and SIGINT receivers. As a result, adversary systems may require less sensitivity to intercept signals and less power to jam them.

- Such platforms are ordinarily at a higher risk for being tracked and targeted by lethal systems.

- The transmission of large amounts of data can potentially compromise the low observability of these platforms.

The integration of ISR and strike platforms is shown in Figure 1.1. There are three main components to this figure. The top band represents space, in which lie ISR satellites (including space-based radar [SBR] or communication satellites) and high-altitude platforms (including U2 and Global Hawk). The middle and lower bands represent medium and low altitudes, in which lie such platforms as fighters, bombers, and smaller unmanned aerial vehicles (UAVs).

It is our assumption that solutions to these challenges, whether technological or related to concepts of operations (CONOPs), are not independent of each other. For instance, in examining options for decreasing the vulnerability of platforms to jamming, it is not sufficient to focus on the merits of individual solutions, such

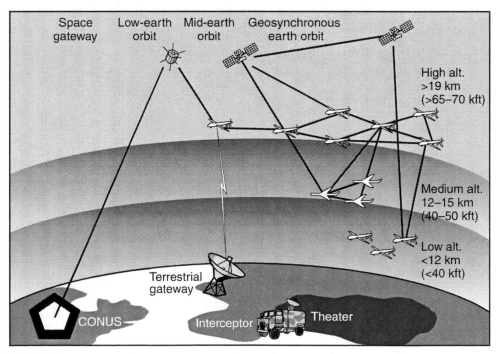

RAND TR159-1.1

Figure 1.1—Integration of ISR and Fighter Platforms

as a narrow mainlobe, higher power, and spread spectrum, without addressing the interrelations or side effects of the options. Such interactions should not be overlooked. For example, it is known that a narrow mainlobe on an antenna may result in higher sidelobes, which increase the observability of the platform, making it more vulnerable.

Adding power to overcome jamming has a similar effect; similarly, spread-spectrum techniques can overcome jamming but may diminish throughput. A number of methods that have been proposed to increase the survivability of the communications network have such undesirable side effects. In this report, we discuss the trade-offs involved in implementing any one or a combination of systems and CONOPs solutions to increase the survivability of the overall communications network.

Organization of This Report

The remainder of this report is divided into four chapters. Chapter 2 discusses our methodology, Chapter 3 explains how we conducted our analysis of the threats from jamming and SIGINT receivers, Chapter 4 presents the main findings of our analysis, and Chapter 5 offers our conclusions and recommendations.

2. Methodology

In this chapter, we explain the key assumptions and limitations of our study. We also describe the threats, requirements, and baselines used in our analysis as well as the systems and programs under review.

Assumptions and Limitations

In our analysis, we assume air superiority in the sense that threats to communications assets are limited to ground jammers and SIGINT receivers.

We focus on high-data-rate networks as they relate to the transmission of sensor data gathered by medium- and low-altitude platforms, because this is the most stressing case. The low-data-rate case is considered to be a lesser-included case.

We focus on the survivability of communications networks against nonlethal systems only, i.e., active jammers and passive SIGINT receivers. Although the latter can affect the survivability of the platform, we do not explicitly address those implications in this phase of our research.

We recognize that no method or technology can make a system completely immune to jamming or interception. The best we can do is to make such threats more difficult and costly for the adversary. In our study, we try to show the degree to which each solution contributes to the survivability of the communications network given our present estimate of the future threat. Although we mention some of the countermeasures an adversary could potentially employ against any of these solutions, detailed analysis of such methods and their effectiveness is beyond the scope of this study.

Threats, Requirements, and Baselines

As noted earlier, we consider two types of threats: mobile ground jammers and ground-based SIGINT receivers. Jammers range from small systems to larger jammers that require large trucks for mobility.

The enemy uses ground-based SIGINT receivers to detect and locate the platform by detecting the signals emitted by these platforms. Unlike jammers, these receivers are silent threats and are therefore difficult to locate. SIGINT receivers range from simple to very sophisticated devices with high sensitivity to signals. These receivers can employ a variety of detectors including: (1) standard radiometers (energy detectors), (2) channelized radiometers, (3) cross-correlators, and (4) compressive receivers. Our analyses are limited to scenarios using a standard radiometer. The others are beyond the scope of this study.

Systems and Programs

We consider a number of current and future systems and programs, as follows:

Joint Tactical Information Distribution System (JTIDS)

JTIDS is a U.S. joint communications service with some secure and jam-resistance capability. The system provides situation awareness and command and control. However, the throughput capacity of this system is only a few kbps, which is not sufficient for the high-data-rate required for sensor data.

Joint Tactical Radio System (JTRS)

JTRS is the future Department of Defense (DoD) radio that will replace the current radio systems, including JTIDS. This program has been developed to address interoperability issues within the military. JTRS is to span a frequency range of 2 MHz to 2 GHz, and it has the potential to increase the transmission frequency to 55 GHz for space communications requirements.

The expected total throughput for JTRS does not provide the high-data-rate required for electro-optical/infrared (EO/IR) sensors.[1] In addition, the level of protection and the low probability of intercept/low probability of detection (LPI/LPD) capabilities are not yet well defined.

We next describe some existing programs and systems that are capable of high-data-rate transmissions and explain their vulnerabilities to various types and levels of threats. We also examine options for increasing the survivability and resilience of the communications links.

---

[1] For more information, see the website at http://jtrs.army.mil/.

The Common Data Link (CDL) Family

The CDL systems and programs described here have high-data-rate capabilities. Although originally designed for ISR platforms, they have the potential to be used on fighter and bomber platforms as well.

The CDL system supports transmit/receive data between airborne ISR platforms and ground processing and combat units, but it is not planned for fighter platforms. The system provides the maximum capacity of 274 Mbps in X- (9.7–10.5 GHz) and Ku- (14.5–15.5 GHz) bands, which is adequate for current communications needs but is not sufficient for the increasing overall communications demand of multi-Gbps.[2] The system is capable of providing some protection against a jamming threat, in which case the data rate falls back to 10 Mbps to increase the link margin for protection. (See more detailed discussion and analysis in Chapters 3 and 4.) The Airborne Information Transmission (ABIT) system offers beyond-line-of-sight range and improved timeliness for real-time operations without burdening already heavily used communications satellites. This system is used on platforms such as U2.

The Tactical Common Data Link (TCDL) system supports air-to-surface transmission of radar, imagery, video, and other sensor information at a range of up to 200 km. This system is used on platforms such as Predator.

Multi-Platform Common Data Link (MP-CDL) is a Concept and Technology Development program that aims to address tactical data link needs. The MP-CDL is a multipoint version of CDL.[3]

These programs can provide high throughput to move imagery and other intelligence information from collection platforms to ground stations and/or other airborne platforms anywhere in the theater. The overall characteristics of these links are summarized in Table 2.1.

---

[2] For more detailed information, please see *Systems Description Document for the Common Data Link System*, May 4, 1998.

[3] For more detailed information, please see *Systems Requirement Document for the Multi-Platform Common Data Link System*, June 11, 2002.

Table 2.1

Systems and Programs

System/Program	Platform	Description
SINCGARS [a] Have Quick	All platforms	Voice
JTIDS JTRS (JTIDS follow-on)	All platforms for JTIDS Up to 5 Mbps	Image up to 5 Mbps network throughput (voice and still images, but not video streaming)
Tactical Targeting Network *Technologies (TTNT)*	*Air-air link*	*10 kbps–Mbps at 100 nm (2 ms)*
Network Centric Collaboration **Targeting (NCCT)**	**Air-air link**	**High data rate 10 Mbps video** **streaming**
Common Data Link **(CDL, MP-CDL)**	**U2, Rivet Joint,** **Global Hawk**	**10, 50, 274 Mbps video streaming**
Airborne Information **Transmission (ABIT)**	**Air-air link**	**10, 50, 274 Mbps**

NOTE: Data rate: Low, *medium*, **high.**

[a] Single-Channel Ground and Airborne Radio System.

Data-Rate Requirement

The data-rate requirement for high-altitude ISR assets is on the order of Gbps, whereas it is on the order of Mbps for medium- and low-altitude platforms with EO/IR and radar capability. The data-rate requirement varies depending on the size and quality of images and the transmission time allowed. For that reason, we take a parametric approach in this study. For the worst-case scenario, we consider the case in which near-real-time transmission speeds are required to support offboard target designation, and the data consist of 1-foot-resolution synthetic aperture images collected by a fourth-generation Active Electronically Scanned Array (AESA) radar. If current-generation G4-class processors are employed, and images are synthesized onboard, we assume a 1.23-Megapixel image can be generated in an interval comparable with the target illumination time. With an advanced processor upgrade, we assume one can generate an image with an area approximately 30 times larger, i.e., about 37 Megapixels. If images are collected at the rate of 1 frame per 30 seconds, and we assume 8 bits per pixel, the data rate required is 10 Mbps. Note that Automatic Target Cueing (ATC) can reduce the transmission requirements by a significant factor, depending on the false-alarm rate. The role of ATC would be to select a few small areas of interest for transmission, one of which is likely to contain the desired target.

Data compression is an effective way to reduce the required transmission time of the platform, thus making it more difficult for the enemy to detect. There are aggressive techniques used in commercial industry that can further compress data by a factor of 8, using the industry standard MPEG2 compression algorithm. However, data compression may result in lower-quality images. For example, a VHS-quality image requires 1.5 Mbps data rate, whereas higher-quality frames such as DVD and HDTV require 6–18 Mbps. In this study, we do not focus on data compression to preserve the high-quality image required for precise target recognition and identification. However, we will study the effect of compression in more detail in future work.

The following chapter discusses the analysis of the threat from jammers and SIGINT receivers. Although CDL family links provide the required data, they have only limited protection against jamming, energy detectors, and radiometers. We discuss this limitation in more detail in Chapter 4.

3. Analysis of Threats from Jamming and SIGINT Receivers

In this chapter, we explain how we calculated the effects of jamming and interception capabilities on communication links. We include the formulas used in our analyses. We also examine the impact of spread spectrum and time-hopping on antijamming and LPI/LPD capability. Nontechnical readers may want to move directly to Chapter 4.

Jamming Analysis

Noise jamming interferes with communications links by increasing the amount of noise present in the receiver. This noise affects the link budget, which is also impacted by other conditions, such as the range between the transmitter and the intended receiver, and atmospheric conditions, such as humidity. The range of mobile jammers in this study is based on an earlier RAND study by Preston et al. (2003).

If one treats jamming as an independent noise source, its effect is to increase the receiver noise floor by the factor $(1 + 10^{JNR/10})$, where JNR is the jamming-to-receiver noise power ratio in dB. Consequently, it reduces the radio frequency (RF) link margin as follows:

$$\text{Margin} = \text{Margin}_0 - 10\log_{10}(1 + 10^{JNR/10}), \tag{1}$$

where Margin_0 represents the nominal margin in the absence of jamming. Margin_0 is given by

$$\text{Margin}_0 \ (dB) = E_{rp} - L_p + Rx_{gain} - Rx_{loss} - N_0 - 10\log_{10} R_b - E_b/N_0, \tag{2}$$

where E_{rp} is the effective radiated power dBm (including transmitter antenna losses and gains); L_p is the propagation loss (dB); $Rx_{gain(loss)}$ denotes the total receiver gain (loss) (dB); N_0 is the receiver noise spectral density (dBm/Hz); R_b is the transmitted (possibly coded) data rate (bps), and E_b/N_0 is the required energy/bit-to-noise spectral density ratio (dB) to achieve a desired bit error rate.

Propagation loss is a function of the range between the transmitter and the receiver, and the radio frequency. Assuming free-space propagation loss, we have the following relationship between receiver range R_I (km), transmitter power P (dBW); transmitter gain G_{TI} (dB) (in the direction of the receiver), and the carrier-to-noise ratio CNR (dB/Hz):

$$P + G_{TI} + 30 - L_{pi} + Rx_{gain} - N_0 = CNR,$$

where Rx_{gain} is the receiver antenna gain (dB); N_0 is the receiver noise spectral density (-170 dBm/Hz assumed in the following);

$$L_{pi} = 92.4 + 20\log_{10}(f) + 20\log_{10}(R_I)$$

is the propagation loss between the transmitter and receiver; and f (GHz) is the operating frequency.

In the following analysis, we focus on line-of-sight links in three frequency bands: X- (8.22 GHz), Ku- (14 GHz), and Ka- (29 GHz) band. For each link, the following assumptions are made: (a) transmit/receive phased-array antennas are used, each with N elements and with 0.75 wavelength spacing between elements; (b) transmitter power is 125 W; (c) -170 dBm/Hz receiver noise spectral level is assumed; and (d) atmospheric-related attenuations are 0 dB at X-band, 1 dB at Ku-band, and 4 dB at Ka-band. Based on data presented in Khatib (1997), the peak gain G_{ant} (dB) of the transmit/receive phased-array antennas is modeled by

$$G_{ant} \approx 9.24 + 10\log_{10}(N \cdot (d / \lambda)^2), \tag{3}$$

where d / λ is the ratio of the array element spacing to the wavelength. Note that G_{ant} enters into the nominal link margin (Eq. 2) via both E_{rp} and Rx_{gain}, and thus, for a fixed d / λ, the nominal link margin increases with increasing N as $20\log_{10} N$.

The corresponding link margins (relative to a nominal E_b / N_0 of 12 dB) are presented in Figures 3.1–3.3. As shown, the link margin decreases with greater frequency because of the additional propagation loss [increasing with frequency f as $20\log_{10}(f)$] as well as the additional assumed atmospheric-related attenuation. Using data presented in Khatib (1997), the estimated payload weights of the transmit/receive phased-array antennas for the different frequency bands and for different values of N are tabulated in Table 3.1.

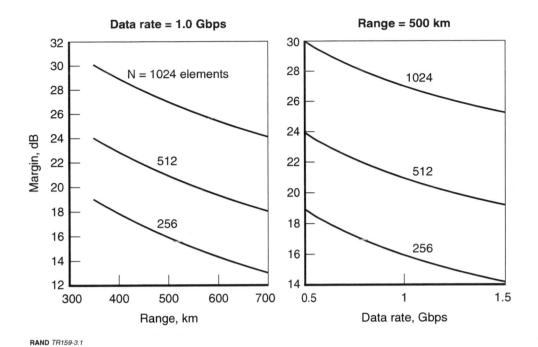

Figure 3.1—X-Band Link Margin

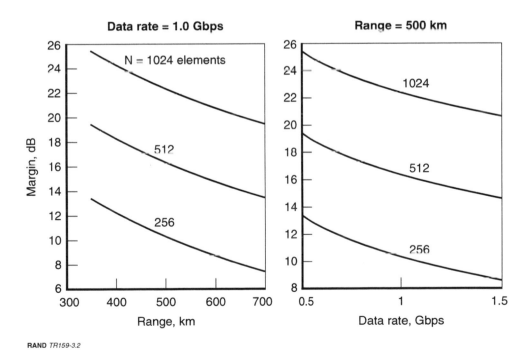

Figure 3.2—Ku-Band Link Margin

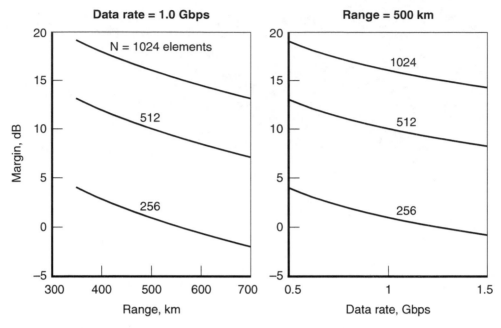

RAND *TR159-3.3*

Figure 3.3—Ka-Band Link Margin

Table 3.1

Estimated Payload Weights for a Single, N-Element Phased-Array Antenna

Frequency Band	N	Weight (lb) [a]
X	250	45
	1500	130
Ku, Ka	250	45
	1500	125
	2000	145

[a] Including controller and power supply.

To parameterize the effects of jamming on system performance, we consider the plane earth[1] geometry depicted in Figure 3.4. For a given altitude H, the jammer range D_J is determined in terms of the elevation angle θ via $D_J = H / \sin\theta$.

___

[1] This is a good approximation over the ranges of interest here.

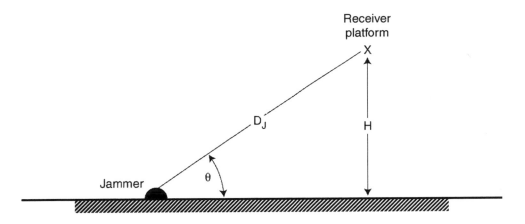

Figure 3.4—Jammer Link Geometry

The received jamming-to-receiver noise power ratio JNR is given by

$$JNR\ (dB) = J_{rp} - L_{pJ} + Rx_{gain;J} - Rx_{loss;J} - N_0 - 10\log_{10} R_b, \tag{4}$$

where J_{rp} denotes the effective radiated power (dBm) from the jammer (including transmitter antenna losses and gains); L_{pJ} is the propagation loss (dB) from the jammer to the receiver platform; $Rx_{gain(loss);J}$ denotes the total receiver gains (losses) (dB) associated with the jammer signal; N_0 is the receiver noise spectral density (dBm/Hz), and R_b is the transmitted data rate (bps). With reference to Figure 3.4, the propagation loss (dB) from the jammer to the receiver L_{pJ} can be expressed in terms of the receiver platform altitude H (km) and the elevation angle θ as

$$L_p = 20\log_{10}(4\pi r f / c) \approx 92.4 + 20\log_{10}(f) + 20\log_{10}(H / \sin\theta), \tag{5}$$

where f is the frequency and $c = 3 \times 10^8\ m/s$ is the speed of light.

Signal Detection Analysis

Detection probability is the probability that a SIGINT receiver will detect an emitter, assuming that the SIGINT receiver antenna is pointed at the emitter. The intercept probability equals detection probability $\times$ time (power on)/receiver scan time.

Probability of Detection (PD) Versus Received Signal Power at the Receiver

Detection, the gateway to interception, includes signal sorting and classification. SIGINT receivers can employ a variety of detectors such as (1) standard radiometers (energy detectors), (2) channelized radiometers, (3) cross-correlators, and (4) compressive receivers. As an illustration of the factors influencing detector performance, we consider a standard radiometer as depicted in Figure 3.5.

The input signal $x(t)$ is first filtered through a predetection filter with a sufficiently wide bandwidth to accommodate the signal class of interest. The predetection filter bandwidth W will typically not be optimized for a given waveform. After predetection filtering, the data $y(t)$ are passed through a square-law device and are then integrated in a postdetection filter over a sufficient time interval T to provide reliable signal threshold detection. The threshold V_T is chosen based on a desired false-alarm probability P_{FA}. Note that a threshold decision can be made every T seconds. Once a signal detection is registered, the other intercept functions are initiated.

The relevant SIGINT receiver parameters include predetection filter bandwidth W; integration time constant T; detection threshold V_T; and false-alarm probability P_{FA}. Other parameters include the received signal power P (at the output of the predetection filter) as well as the receiver spectral noise density N_0. The former depends upon the radiated source power in the direction of the receiver; the range from the source to the receiver; the operating frequency f_0; and the antenna gain of the receiver in the direction of the source. The receiver spectral noise density N_0 is dependent upon the receiver noise figure F.

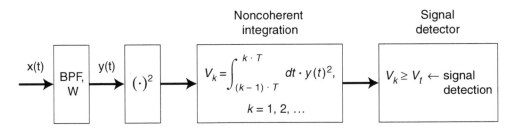

RAND *TR159-3.5*

Figure 3.5—Energy Detector

Assuming the receiver noise is spectrally white and Gaussian, then the probability of signal detection P_D is given by [Torrieri, 1985]:

$$P_D = \frac{1}{2} \int\limits_{2V_T/N_0}^{\infty} dx \cdot \left(\frac{x}{\lambda}\right)^{(\gamma-1)/2} \cdot \exp(-\frac{x+\lambda}{2}) \cdot I_{\gamma-1}(\sqrt{x\lambda}), \tag{1a}$$

where γ denotes the largest integer not exceeding the time-bandwidth product $T \cdot W$, i.e., $\gamma \rfloor \lfloor T \cdot W \rfloor$; $I_{\gamma-1}(\cdot)$ is the modified Bessel function of the first kind and order $\gamma - 1$; $\lambda \rfloor 2 \cdot P \cdot T / N_0$ is twice the intercepted signal energy-to-noise spectral density ratio, and V_T / N_0 can be directly related to P_{FA} via:

$$P_{FA} = \exp\left(-\frac{V_T}{N_0}\right) \cdot \sum_{k=0}^{\gamma-1} \frac{1}{k!} \cdot \left(\frac{V_T}{N_0}\right)^k. \tag{1b}$$

Thus, given P_{FA}, V_T / N_0 can be obtained by inverting Eq. (1b).

Two limiting cases are worth noting: large $T \cdot W$ and $T \cdot W = 1$. In the former case, V_k (Figure 3.5) is approximately Gaussian and we have the approximations for P_D and P_{FA} [Torrieri, 1985]:

$$P_D = \frac{1}{2} \cdot erfc\left[\frac{V_T / N_0 - T \cdot W - \lambda/2}{\sqrt{2 \cdot (T \cdot W + \lambda)}}\right], \tag{2a}$$

and

$$P_{FA} = \frac{1}{2} \cdot erfc\left[\frac{V_T / N_0 - T \cdot W}{\sqrt{2 \cdot T \cdot W}}\right], \tag{2b}$$

where $erfc(\cdot)$ is the complementary error function defined by

$$erfc(x) \rfloor \frac{2}{\sqrt{\pi}} \cdot \int\limits_{x}^{\infty} du \cdot \exp(-u^2). \tag{2c}$$

This is a reasonable approximation for detecting spread-spectrum transmissions. Given $N_{0=}170$,

$$P_s \ (dBm) = CNR \ (dB-Hz) + N_0 = CNR - 170.$$

Plots of R_I versus data rate are presented in Figure 3.6 for different G_{TI} and for $CNR = 49$ dB-Hz ($T = 100$ sec, single-channel radiometer) and $CNR = 31$ dB/Hz ($T = 1$ sec). As is seen with a $T = 1$ sec radiometer integration, the link becomes quite vulnerable to long-range interception ($R_I > 100$ km) at data rates on the order of 1 Mbps once G_{TI} exceeds -10 dB.

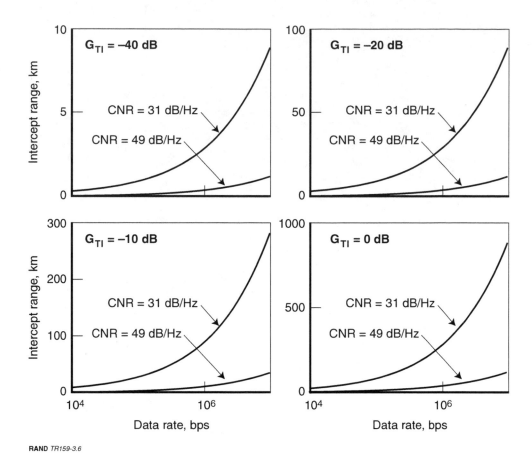

RAND *TR159-3.6*

Figure 3.6—Intercept Ranges as a Function of Transmitted Data Rate

Based on the single-channel radiometer detectability analysis carried out previously, we consider here trade-offs between received signal level P_s, predetection resolution bandwidth B, and detector integration time $T = K / B$, where $K = B \cdot T$ is the detector time-bandwidth product. In this analysis, it is assumed that the SIGINT receiver spectral noise density is a nominal $N_0 = -170$ dBm/Hz. It is further assumed that the communication link becomes vulnerable once the detection probability P_D exceeds 10^{-6} at a false-alarm probability P_{FA} of 10^{-8}.

Given that detectability can be conveniently parameterized in terms of the signal power-to-noise spectral density ratio $CNR = P_s / N_0$ at the intercept receiver, then for a given N_0 we can equivalently parameterize detector performance in terms of

$$P_s \ (dBm) = CNR \ (dB - Hz) + N_0 \ = CNR - 170 \ .$$

To compute the signal-to-noise ratio and bandwidth, we use formulas (2a), (2b), and (2c) above, which provide approximations for P_D and P_{FA}. Given $P_D = 10^{-6}$ and $P_{FA} = 10^{-8}$, we note that

$$\frac{1}{2} \cdot erfc\left[3.35\right] \sim P_D \tag{3a}$$

and

$$\frac{1}{2} \cdot erfc\left[3.96\right] \sim P_{FA}. \tag{3b}$$

Substituting into Eqs. (2a) and (2b), we derive the following relationship between K, B, and CNR (valid for large K):

$$
\begin{aligned}
K &\sim 2 \cdot \left(3.96 \cdot B / CNR - 3.35 \cdot (B / CNR) \cdot \sqrt{1 + 2 \cdot CNR / B}\right)^2 \\
&\sim 2 \cdot \left(3.96 \cdot B / CNR - 3.35 \cdot (B / CNR) \cdot (1 + CNR / B)\right)^2 \\
&= 2 \cdot \left(0.61 \cdot B / CNR - 3.35\right)^2,
\end{aligned}
\tag{4}
$$

where we make the assumption (second equality in (2a)) that $CNR / B \ll 1$ (which is valid for large B). Given Eq. (4), we can plot P_s for different values of B and T.

The carpet plot in Figure 3.7 corresponds to the nominal detection parameters. The predetection resolution bandwidth B is typically chosen to span the widest possible signal bandwidth of interest. As seen in the figure, for a given T, increasing B results in larger signal detection thresholds. For example, at $T = 1$ sec, the minimum detectable signal level is approximately –140 dBm at $B = 1$ MHz; however, at $B = 100$ MHz, the minimum detectable signal level increases to almost –130 dBm. This illustrates the importance of spread-spectrum waveforms, which force the SIGINT receiver to increase B and thereby degrade its signal detection threshold.

Furthermore, keeping the average transmitted message as short as possible limits the SIGINT receiver's maximum effective integration time T and therefore also degrades its signal detection threshold. For example, at $B = 1$ MHz, a signal detection threshold of approximately –145 dBm is feasible if $T = 10$ sec, whereas this increases to almost –130 dBm if the SIGINT receiver is forced to reduce T to only 10 msec (or equivalently if the average message duration is reduced to 10 msec, which is possible for command/control data transmissions).

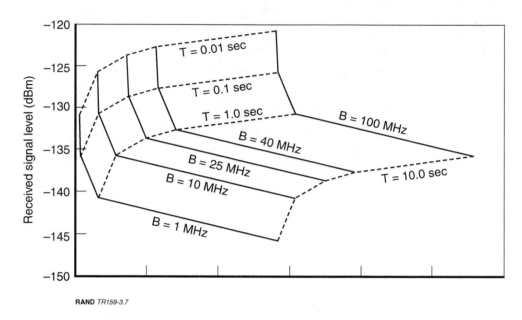

RAND *TR159-3.7*

Figure 3.7—Single-Channel Radiometer Intercept Carpet Plot Corresponding to
Detector Parameters $P_D = 10^{-6}$, $P_{FA} = 10^{-8}$, and $N_0 = -170$ dBm/Hz

Chapter 4 discusses the results of our analysis.

4. Options to Mitigate Jamming and Increase LPI/LPD

Moderate jammers and SIGINT receivers are serious threats to communication networks. In addition, the survivability of the entire platform can be compromised if the enemy uses SIGINT receivers to detect and locate air platforms. To guard against these threats, it is critical to improve existing antijam and low-probability of intercept/low probability of detection (LPI/LPD) capabilities in the communications network.

In this chapter, we examine the feasibility of the following options for these purposes:

- Spread spectrum and frequency-hopping
- Smart antennae
- Absorption band
- Free space laser.

The CDL Family Provides an Adequate Capacity and Some Protection Against Detection and Jamming, But It May Not Be Enough

As explained earlier, CDL and MP-CDL are capable of providing the data rate required for transmitting sensor data from fighter and bomber platforms with high-resolution sensor capabilities. Figure 4.1 illustrates the trade-off among the data rate, antenna size, and the range between the receiver and transmitter. For example, a 48-in. antenna aperture, such as the one on Global Hawk, can support up to a 50-Mbps link from the airborne platform to a satellite. Similarly, a 9-in. aperture, similar to that on the Predator package, can support a long-range air-to-air link.

CDL family links degrade rather gracefully in a hostile jamming environment. The throughput degrades from 270 Mbps to 10 Mbps to increase the margin by about 14 dB. This margin provides some protection against jamming, which we will discuss. However, these links are not designed for more severe jamming environments or SIGINT receivers.

22

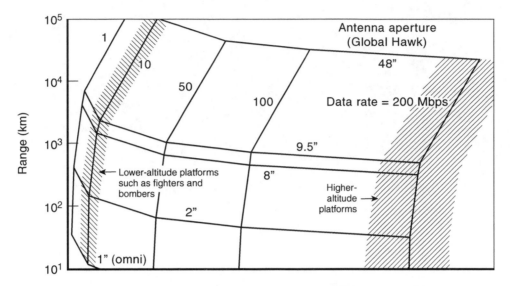

NOTE: Assumptions: 10-dB margin air-to-air link (over 12-dB Eb/N_0): air CDL link (AT-100) transmit/receive antennas with 200-W radiated power; 15 GHz.
RAND *TR159-4.1*

Figure 4.1—Antenna Size, Data Rate, and Link Range Trade-Offs

Spreading the Signal Over Time and Bandwidth Increases LPI/LPD But Degrades Link Capacity

Spread-spectrum techniques produce LPI signals that are difficult to detect, read, or jam. These techniques spread the energy of the transmitted signal across a frequency band that is much wider than is normally required. This approach makes the location of the transmitter difficult to detect.

By introducing a duty cycle (on-off transmission pattern, random or periodic), the communicator spreads its transmissions over time much like frequency-hopping or spread-spectrum modulation spreads the transmission over frequency; this technique is known as time-hopping. If one assumes that the SIGINT receiver is not smart enough to synchronize to the transmissions, then the receiver is forced to integrate over a long time interval T in an attempt to collect enough energy to determine whether or not the communicator is transmitting.

Again, this approach is analogous to spread-spectrum communications wherein the SIGINT receiver is forced to use a wider bandwidth to collect all of the transmitted energy from the communicator. The net effect of this is to lower the average intercepted power by a factor alpha, which is the ratio of total transmission time T_s to T, i.e.,

$$\text{duty cycle} = \alpha = T_s/T.$$

Thus, the average intercepted power is reduced by alpha over what would be received if the communicator were transmitting continuously (at peak power). The received signal level at the SIGINT receiver is reduced by 10*(log10(alpha)).

Smart Antennae Increase Jam Resistance

Smart antenna processing reduces the effect of jamming by placing antenna nulls in the direction of the jammer to cancel its effect. Smart antenna processing systems range from simple sidelobe cancellers to more sophisticated, multielement, phased-array antennae. In the case of sidelobe canceling, jamming energy received through the sidelobe of the primary antenna (phased array, dish, etc.) is cancelled via an auxiliary antenna (phased array, omnidirectional antenna element, reflector, etc.), which is (ideally) shielded from the incident jamming signal of interest. Multielement phased arrays use adaptive beamforming networks to provide jammer cancellation, as noted above.

In any case, the reduction in jamming effect afforded by smart antenna processing depends on several factors, including platform dynamics, total number of antenna elements available, and number of active jammers. Typical airborne smart-antenna processing systems can provide an additional 20 to 60 dB of cancellation in jamming-to-receiver noise power over that provided from the sidelobe antenna gain of the primary antenna pattern.

Figure 4.2 is another carpet plot illustrating the trade-offs between the size (i.e., the number of elements in the phased-array antenna), data rate, and range between transmitter and receiver. As an example, this figure illustrates how 256-element antennae at both a receiver and transmitter can support a 30-Mbps data rate up to 200 km.

LPI/LPD Antenna Design Can Protect Against Silent Threats and a Severe Jamming Environment

As discussed above, the smart antenna increases antijam capability. However, it does not provide protection against SIGINT receivers such as a standard radiometer (energy detector). This problem can be addressed through antenna designs aimed at lowering the signal received by a SIGINT receiver. The probability of detection can be substantially decreased by reducing power and sidelobes.

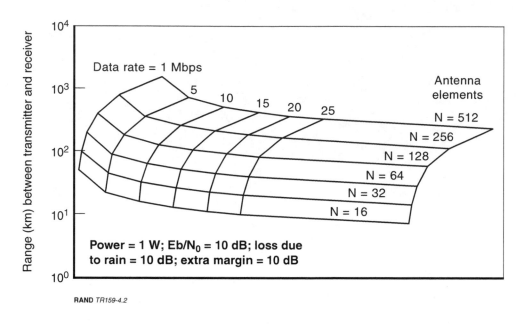

RAND *TR159-4.2*

Figure 4.2—Phased-Array Antenna Receiver Based on Link Range and Data Rate

SIGINT receivers are more effective in detecting the mainlobe of an antenna, which emits more energy. It is obviously desirable to keep the main beam off the ground. Figure 4.3 illustrates a communication beam from a fighter to other platforms at the higher altitudes such as ISR and communication nodes.

To avoid ground interception, the beamwidth should remain narrow. However, the maximum width of the beam is relative to the altitude of the transmitter and receiver. Higher-altitude platforms can enjoy a wider beamwidth and avoid ground threats. Figure 4.4 illustrates the trade-off between the altitude and the range between the platforms versus the beamwidth. For longer-range communications, the width of the beam should be narrower to avoid ground illumination. On the left side of Figure 4.4, we consider a range of platforms, from medium-altitude platforms, such as some fighters, to higher-altitude platforms, such as ISR platforms and/or communication relays at 20 km. As illustrated, the link range cannot exceed 100 km and maintain a 20-deg null-to-null beamwidth.

The carpet plot on the right side of the figure illustrates the same information for platforms at the same altitude, such as fighter-to-fighter or ISR-to-ISR platforms. The figure illustrates range versus altitude versus beamwidth. For lower-altitude platforms, such as fighters, this technique may not be effective because the null-to-null beamwidth would have to be impossibly narrow. For example, for the platforms at 6 km, the null-to-null beamwidth should be less than 3 deg for ranges up to 250 km.

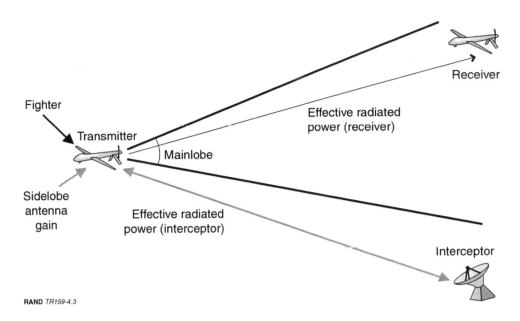

RAND *TR159-4.3*

Figure 4.3—Protecting Against Silent Threat

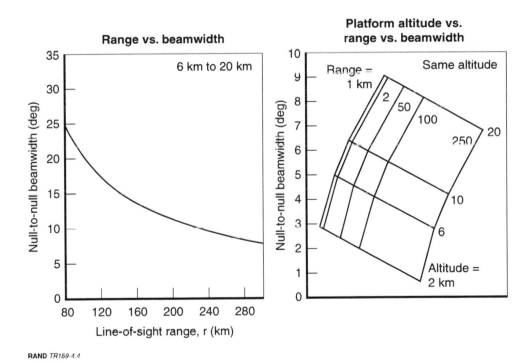

RAND *TR159-4.4*

Figure 4.4—Maximum Beamwidth Allowable for Keeping the Main Beam Off the Ground

Outside the main beam of the antennae are the sidelobes, which are an undesirable—but unavoidable—feature, especially in this case. Sidelobes have to be suppressed as much as possible; however, suppressing sidelobes usually degrades antenna efficiency and increases the beamwidth. Thus, to maintain high gain in the mainlobe and keep the beamwidth narrow, the antenna size has to be increased (Georgia Institute of Technology, 1993). Figure 4.5 illustrates the trade-off between beamwidth sidelobe and antenna size. The figure indicates that a 20-deg null-to-null corresponds to a 21-in. antenna diameter for a 48-dB sidelobe reduction.

Spread-Spectrum, Low-Power, Low-Sidelobe Techniques Can Be Combined for Intratheater Platforms

Our analysis to evaluate the adequacy of current systems in a severe jamming environment found that the current systems are not adequate for robust communications. To address the challenges posed by a more severe jamming environment, a combination of spread spectrum and phased-array antennas with nulling capabilities will be required.

The options we have discussed can help reduce vulnerabilities in the communications network, but each option has its unique limitations. Spread spectrum alone does not protect against more-advanced jammers. Because spread-spectrum techniques use a high percentage of bandwidth, these techniques are not very useful for higher data rates. Antijam capabilities can be increased by increasing the effective radiated power, but LPI/LPD will be diminished as a result.

Maintaining the balance between antenna power and LPI/LPD requires a combination of directionality, power management, and low sidelobes. The first option for achieving LPD is to decrease the antenna's effective radiated power (ERP) in the direction of energy detectors. However, because SIGINT receiver threats are hard to locate, it will also be necessary to keep the mainlobe off the ground (in case of ground threats) and reduce the sidelobes. This technique is useful primarily for platforms at altitudes of 12 km and above. Using different types of tapers can reduce the antenna sidelobe. However, the use of tapers will increase antenna size while decreasing its efficiency. For example, a 256-element antenna on both receiver and transmitter can support 10-Mbps data rate at a range of 250 km. However, to reduce sidelobes sufficiently to maintain an "acceptable" protection against energy detectors, a much larger antenna would be needed. In this example, a 512-element antenna would be required to achieve a 25-dB (from the peak mainlobe) gain reduction in sidelobes (using Blackman taper) while maintaining a null-null 20-deg beamwidth.

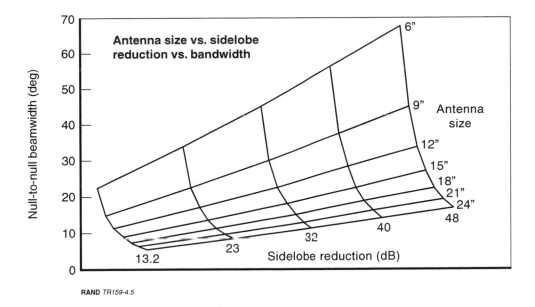

Figure 4.5—Suppressing Sidelobe Increases Antenna Size

The carpet plot in Figure 4.6 illustrates the trade-offs between three parameters: (1) range or distance between the SIGINT receiver and the transmitter, (2) ERP in the direction of the SIGINT receiver, and (3) SIGINT receiver sensitivity, ranging from very moderate current receivers with –50-dBm sensitivity to very advanced receivers with –140 dBm.

A moderate SIGINT receiver can easily detect a Global Hawk-type antenna with an ERP of 70 dBm at the mainlobe. As is illustrated in Figure 4.6, a moderate receiver can easily detect this type of antenna even from its sidelobes (with –50-dBm sensitivity). Suppressing the sidelobes, however, decreases the received signal at the SIGINT receiver. A current state-of-the-art SIGINT receiver (with –100-dBm sensitivity) would still be able to intercept such a signal. Additional spreading and time-hopping reduces the signal effectiveness at the SIGINT receiver.

The current CDL program, which uses a parabolic dish, can be susceptible to severe jamming. Although a comparable parabolic antenna dish can support the same link, it may not provide the required jamming protection. We therefore examined the levels of protection provided by different antenna options against various mobile jammers.

28

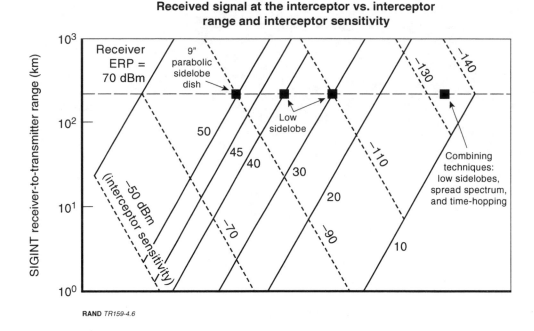

Received signal at the interceptor vs. interceptor range and interceptor sensitivity

RAND *TR159-4.6*

Figure 4.6—Transmitter ERP in the Direction of SIGINT Receiver vs. Intercept Sensitivity and Range

Figure 4.7 illustrates link range versus jammer range. Four levels of jamming threats are analyzed, from more severe in the upper left corner to less severe in the lower left corner.[1] The analysis assumed that stationary ground jammers could be detected and destroyed. In the figure, a 30-dB protection line corresponds to a 512-element receiver antenna gain (in the direction of transmitter).

As demonstrated in the lower left corner of the figure, without further protection, a moderate mobile jammer (63 dBW) would be capable of jamming a link even from a long range. As we explained earlier, spread-spectrum techniques can provide additional protection against jamming; however, they also degrade link capacity. By reducing the data rate to 2 MHz and spreading

---

[1] Platforms are considered to be operating at 20-km altitude at Ku-band with 10-dB rain attenuation. Transmitter ERP is 30 dB (corresponding to 512 elements), 20-dB jammer antenna gain, 10-mbps data rate, 18-dB link SNR (corresponding to a 6-dB margin over Eb/No = 12 dB).

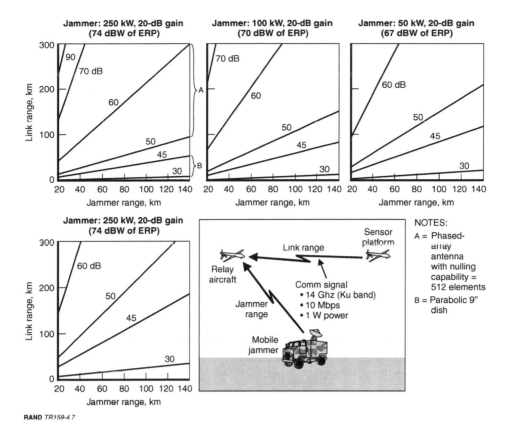

Figure 4.7—Link Range vs. Jammer Range for Various Jammer Transmit Powers and Gain (i.e., Jammer ERP)

the signal over 250 MHz, an additional ~20-dB protection can be obtained. A total of 50 dB appears to provide adequate protection for short-range (<20-km) links.

For longer-range links, the antijam capability can be further enhanced through the use of a phased-array antenna with nulling capability. The combination of nulling, spread spectrum, and receiver gain can provide ~90-dB protection. This level of protection provides robust long-range communications even with more-powerful directional jammers of 74-dBW ERP, as shown in the upper left corner of Figure 4.7.

Obviously, a higher-gain antenna with increased nulling capability provides greater robustness and increased capacity. The cost of such an improvement may be mitigated by using a more-advanced existing antenna for imaging.

Robustness can also be enhanced through use of stealthy platforms. Directional jammers become ineffective if they are unable to track and point the receiver platform. A stealthy platform degrades directional jammer capability to track and point and hence degrades their effectiveness. Further analysis is required to examine the effectiveness of this option.

Absorption Band Is a Viable Option for the Backbone Network But Not for Long-Range Intratheater Links

Communications in the absorption band [55–65 GHz] provide a wider bandwidth but also provide substantial atmospheric attenuation of a ground-based jamming threat when the air platforms are operating at high altitudes (i.e., 20 km or greater).

Atmospheric absorption makes the absorption band very unattractive for communication links in the troposphere. The atmospheric attenuation at 10 km is about 10 times higher (i.e., 4–5 dB/km) than that at 20 km. As a consequence, the integrated attenuation for the link accumulates much faster than it does for the higher-altitude backbone links, thus making use of the absorption band impractical for long-range links.

A Laser Communication System Is the Most Robust Link Above the Cloud Level

So far, we have focused on improving capacity and providing antijamming protection for communications links using radio frequencies. However, the high carrier frequency and bandwidth potential of laser optics offers several potential advantages over RF links: much higher data rates, reduced payload weights and power consumption, increased covertness, and reduced vulnerability to jamming. Optical links can also operate in parallel with other assets, because they do not use the same allocated and regulated spectrum as RF communications. Laser optics efficiently and simultaneously transfer multiple wideband channels and allow the data to be encoded, decoded, and routed to many users via a single transceiver system. Laser optics are of particular interest to military users because of their narrow transmit beams, which have very low sidelobe levels and thereby provide a very low probability of intercept.

Optical links have a number of disadvantages, however. A fundamental problem is that rain and clouds, which absorb laser beams, significantly degrade communications. Because cloud formation is usually limited to altitudes below 12 km, absorption is less of a problem for high-altitude platforms. Another concern is that the highly directed transmit beams coupled with the vibration of satellites and platforms pose difficulties in tracking, acquiring, and maintaining the link.

These limitations might be overcome through a combination of laser optics technology and RF technologies capable of increasing covert high-data-rate communications. The RF technology could be used to receive and transmit communications to a ground station in the presence of clouds, and laser optics could be used for high-altitude (above the cloud level) air-to-air, air-to-satellite, and satellite-to-satellite and air- or satellite-to-ground links in dry climates. Although laser optic technology is still in development and therefore poses implementation risks, there is evidence that these problems may be resolved in the near future. The Optical Communications Technology group at Lincoln Laboratory has been developing the system concepts and space-qualified hardware to build a package that could support high-data-rate optical links. Based on their results, the group concluded that the current technology is ready for an operational system with a satellite-to-satellite link capability of several hundred megabits per second, and that this number would increase to multiple gigabits in the near future.[2]

A congressionally mandated and funded program known as the Recce.Intel Laser Crosslink Program started in 1996 with the objective of demonstrating full duplex air-to-air lasercom using autonomous signal acquisition and tracking with the terminal and other hardware. AFRL has estimated an operational UAV optical terminal at less than 150 lbs.

---

[2] Interview with Roy Bondurant at Massachusetts Institute of Technology, Cambridge, MA, 2002; and with Hamid Hemmati at Jet Propulsion Laboratory, Pasadena, CA, 2002. See also Hemmati (2002).

5. The Answer Is in the Combination

As the analysis in the previous chapter has suggested, there is no one solution for all situations and platforms. Options for a reliable and robust communications link may change depending on altitude, range, data rate, and threat.

The main findings of this study are illustrated in Figure 5.1.

In summary:

- JTIDS and future JTRS do not have the required capacity to support the high-data-rate connectivity requirement.

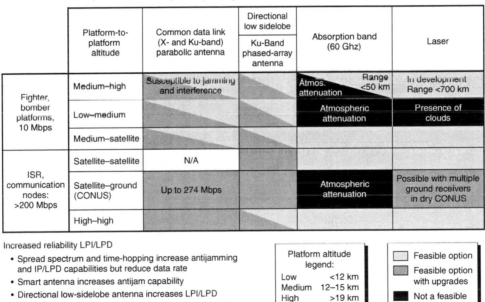

Figure 5.1—Wideband Communications Options: New Systems Will Be Required

- CDL-family programs can provide a sufficient data rate for the fighter/bomber with Advanced Synthetic Aperture Radar System (ASARS)–Improved Program (AIP) capability. However, these systems need further improvement to survive a severe threat environment.
  - Spread spectrum can provide some protection against jamming, but it reduces the data rate.
  - A near-term solution for improving jam resistance is to add nulling capability to CDL families (including MP-CDL). However, although nulling techniques are effective for jammers, they are not effective against SIGINT receivers such as energy detectors.
  - Agile, multibeam, low-sidelobe directional antennae are required to achieve more protection against jamming and SIGINT receivers. These techniques increase the size and weight of the antenna.
- High-altitude platforms, such as ISR platforms, communication nodes and satellites, have two communications options:
  - This absorption band is a viable option for links above 60,000 ft (ISR and communication nodes).
  - Laser is the most robust option for links above 40,000 ft.
- Proliferated platforms with multiple beams, in principle, may form a more robust, reliable network. Further analysis is required to examine the effectiveness of such platforms.

Thus, communication does not appear to be a major limiting factor, at least not technically, in developing future ISR forces. However, programmatic action will be required to develop the necessary systems, and the costs could be significant. The communications problems posed by future ISR forces appear solvable, but at a cost.

Bibliography

Georgia Institute of Technology, *Antenna Engineering Handbook*, Richard C. Johnson and Henry Jasik (eds.), 1st ed., New York: McGraw-Hill, Inc., 1993.

Hemmati, Hamid, *Status of Free-Space Optical Communications Program at JPL*, Pasadena, Calif.: Jet Propulsion Laboratory, 2000.

Joint Tactical Radio System (JTRS), accessed online at http://jtrs.army.mil/

Khatib, H. H., "Theater Wideband Communications," *1997 MILCOM Proceedings*, November 2–5, 1997, pp. 378–382.

Preston, Bob, Rosalind Lewis, David Frelinger, and Alexander Hou, *Protecting the Military Utility of U.S. Space Systems*, Santa Monica, Calif.: RAND Corporation, MR-1512-AF, 2003 (document not available to the general public).

Systems Description Document for the Common Data Link System, May 4, 1998.

Systems Requirement Document for the Multi-Platform Common Data Link System, June 11, 2002.

Torrieri, D., *Principles of Secure Communication Systems*, Dedham, Mass.: Artech House, 1985.